Good Housekeeping Cookery Club

FISH & SHELLFISH

Jacqueline Clarke

TED SMART

A TED SMART Publication 1995

1 3 5 7 9 10 8 6 4 2

First published in the United Kingdom in 1994 by Ebury Press
Random House, 20 Vauxhall Bridge Road, London SW1V 2SA

Random House Australia (Pty) Limited
20 Alfred Street, Milsons Point, Sydney,
New South Wales 2061, Australia

Random House New Zealand Limited
18 Poland Road, Glenfield,
Auckland 10, New Zealand

Random House South Africa (Pty) Limited
PO Box 337, Bergvlei, South Africa

Random House UK Limited Reg. No. 954009

A CIP catalogue record for this book is available from the British Library.

Managing Editor: JANET ILLSLEY
Design: SARA KIDD
Special Photography: JAMES MURPHY
Food Stylist: ALLYSON BIRCH
Photographic Stylist: ROISIN NIELD
Techniques Photography: KARL ADAMSON
Food Techniques Stylist: ANGELA KINGSBURY
Recipe Testing: EMMA-LEE GOW

ISBN 0 09 180550 3

Typeset in Gill Sans by SX Composing Ltd, Rayleigh, Essex
Colour Separations by Magnacraft, London
Printed and bound in Italy by New Interlitho Italia S.p.a., Milan

CONTENTS

COOKERY NOTES

- Both metric and imperial measures are given for the recipes. Follow either metric or imperial throughout as they are not interchangeable.
- All spoon measures are level unless otherwise stated. Sets of measuring spoons are available in both metric and imperial for accurate measurement of small quantities.
- Ovens should be preheated to the specified temperature. Grills should also be preheated. The cooking times given in the recipes assume that this has been done.
- Where a stage is specified in brackets under freezing instructions, the dish should be frozen at the end of that stage.
- Size 2 eggs should be used except where otherwise specified. Free-range eggs are recommended.
- Use freshly ground black pepper and sea salt unless otherwise specified.
- Use fresh rather than dried herbs unless dried herbs are suggested in the recipe
- Stocks should be freshly made if possible. Alternatively buy ready-made stocks or use good quality stock cubes.

INTRODUCTION

Fish and shellfish have always been great favourites of mine. From prawns eaten on summer holidays many years ago in Cornwall, to canned tuna fish and fresh mussels – staples through student days in Brighton – to fresh oysters devoured during recent holidays in France. In my home town of Dundee, Scotland, I have always been fortunate enough to enjoy the freshest and best cod, haddock, salmon and sea trout.

From a nutritional point of view, fish is excellent. It's low in unsaturated fat, full of protein and contains calcium, iron and vitamin B.

The most important consideration when choosing and buying fish and shellfish is freshness. The natural colours of the fish should be as vibrant as when it left the water, the eyes bright and the gills a vivid red. The fish should feel stiff to the touch and smell like a whiff of sea air, with a slight hint of iodine. If it passes the test, your chosen variety is fresh and ready to cook. Ideally fish should be cooked on the day you purchase it, but it can be stored, well wrapped, in the refrigerator for up to 24 hours.

Preparing fish is relatively easy, especially if you use the illustrated step-by-step guide to basic preparation methods on the following pages. All that is required is a little patience and practice. However, if you are not keen, a good fishmonger should be willing to carry out most of these tasks for you. Remember to ask for the heads, bones and trimmings to make into stock, either for immediate use in the recipe, or to freeze for the future.

When buying shellfish, look for those with tightly closed shells. Scallops, mussels, clams and oysters are still alive when sold fresh and any sign of an open shell may indicate that the specimen is far from fresh. Sometimes a sharp tap on the shell may persuade the shellfish to close up, telling you that he's alive and kicking, but if not, you should certainly avoid it!

When buying cooked shellfish, such as lobster, crab and prawns, make sure the shells are intact. They should feel quite heavy, and again have an agreeable smell.

Fish is relatively quick to cook – whichever method you use. A fish steak or fillet pan-fried or grilled with a little butter, lemon juice and seasoning is ideal 'fast food', but without the 'junk food' connotation. Grilling and pan-frying are also good for small fish, such as sardines, herring and red mullet, all of which just need the merest lick of oil or butter.

Cooking fish on a griddle pan – a flat cast-iron pan with ridges – is another excellent quick method. It's best applied to firmer fish, such as monkfish, tuna, scallops, squid and whole prawns, which will hold together over the high heat. This method produces attractive criss-cross markings on the fish.

Deep-frying is suited to small fish, such as whitebait and baby squid, which can be cooked whole. Cutlets and fillets can be deep-fried too.

Normally the fish is first coated in breadcrumbs, seasoned flour or batter, which forms a crisp, protective coating against the hot fat, keeping the fish inside moist.

Poaching is perfect for larger whole fish such as salmon, salmon trout and sea bass. The fish is gently simmered in a court bouillon or broth, then left to cool in the liquid, ensuring tender, moist flesh. Cutlets and fillets can also be poached.

Cooking fish 'en papillote', in a sealed parcel of paper or foil, is perfect for small whole fish, cutlets and fillets. The fish is cooked in its own steam with herbs, spices, a flavoured butter or citrus juice added, to impart flavour and create a wonderful aroma when the parcel is opened. This is a good one to impress dinner party guests!

Steaming is a simple and healthy way of cooking fish, suitable for whole fish, steaks and fillets. Braising – on a bed of vegetables in a sealed pan – is another good method, especially suited to firm, meaty fish, such as monkfish or tuna. Fish fillets and steaks of uniform thickness also cook successfully in the microwave.

The variety of fish and shellfish available to us now is quite astounding – from exotic shark steaks and parrot fish to our own salmon, haddock and cod.

I hope this book will inspire you to take a fresh look at fish, and tempt you to include it in your diet on a frequent and regular basis. After all, few things could be better for you!

PREPARATION TECHNIQUES

Prepare and cook fish and shellfish as soon as possible after purchase. Note that once fish has been cut into fillets or steaks it is liable to deteriorate more rapidly.

PREPARING SCALLOPS

1. Scrub the shells under cold running water. Give any that are open a sharp tap with the back of a knife. Discard any that do not close.

2. Hold a scallop flat-side up in the palm of your hand. Insert the point of a strong medium-sized knife between the shells at about 45° to the hinge. It probably won't go straight in but continue pushing and twisting until it does.

3. When the shells have opened slightly, slide your finger in between the shells (it's a good idea to wear a sturdy glove for this) then with the knife in your other hand, quickly cut round the top shell to sever the muscle and allow the shells to be parted.

4. Push the top shell backwards until the hinge at the back snaps. Rinse the scallop (still attached to the lower shell) under cold running water.

5. Using a small knife and being careful not to tear the flesh, cut away the grey beard-like fringe.

6. Slide the point of a knife under the black thread on the side of the scallop. Gently pull it off with the attached intestinal bag and discard. Ease the scallop away from the bottom shell. Slice the scallop meat into rounds if required.

PREPARING MUSSELS

1. Put the mussels in the sink and under cold running water scrape off any mud or barnacles with a sharp knife. Pull away the hair-like beard that protrudes from the shell.

2. Tap any mussels that remain open with the back of the knife. If they refuse to close, throw them away. Rinse again in cold water until there is no trace of sand.

PREPARING LARGE PRAWNS (RAW OR COOKED)

1. Grip head between thumb and forefinger. Gently pull until it comes off, holding tail shell with the other hand.

2. Peel off the body shell and legs.

3. Large prawns have a bitter tasting intestinal vein running down their back. Remove this with a sharp knife and discard.

PREPARING CRAB

Extracting the meat from a cooked crab is time-consuming but well worth the effort. Aim to keep separate the brown body meat, which is mostly liver, the flaky white meat and the creamy body meat.

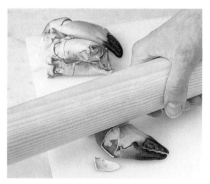

1. Twist off the legs and claws as close to the body as possible. Break each claw in half, then crack with a rolling pin or hammer without crushing the flesh. Break the shell on the legs with your hands. Using a slender skewer to reach awkward bits, carefully extract the flesh.

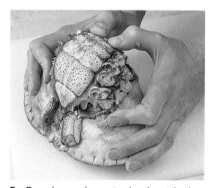

2. Put the crab on its back with the tail flap pointing towards you. Holding the shell firmly, press the body section upwards with your thumbs and it should come away. If it won't move, use the point of a rigid knife to ease it away.

PREPARING LOBSTER

3. With a teaspoon scoop out into separate bowls the creamy meat and roe (if any) from the shell. Remove and discard the stomach bag which you will find between the eyes. (If this breaks make sure you remove all the greenish or grey-white matter.)

1. Twist off the claws and pincers. Crack open the large claws using the back of a heavy knife, being careful not to crush the meat inside. Reserve the smaller claws to use as a garnish.

3. Remove and discard the intestinal vein from the tail, the stomach (which lies near the head) and the inedible gills or 'dead man's fingers'.

4. Pull away from the body and discard the inedible feathery gills or 'dead man's fingers'. Using a large heavy knife, cut the body in half. Using a skewer, remove the flesh from the tiny crevices.

2. Put the lobster, back upwards, on a flat surface and using a sharp knife split the lobster cleanly in two, piercing through the 'cross' at the centre of the head.

4. Using a teaspoon, scoop out the edible soft grey liver (tomalley) and red roe (if any). Carefully lift the tail meat from the shell, pulling it out in one piece.

5. Using a skewer, carefully remove the meat from the legs.

SKINNING FISH

If you're intending to cook flat fish whole, remove the dark skin only; the white skin will hold the fish in one piece during cooking. Flat fish that are to be filleted should be skinned completely. Round fish and very large flat fish are easier to skin after filleting or cooking.

TO SKIN FLAT FISH

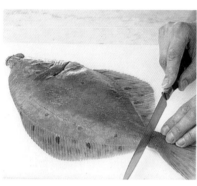

1. Lay the fish on a board, dark side uppermost, and make an incision across the skin where the tail joins the body. Use the point of the knife to lift a flap of skin.

2. Grasp the flap of skin with your salted fingers and, holding down the tail in the other hand, pull the skin away cleanly in one piece. Turn the fish over and remove the white skin, if desired.

BONING AND FILLETING FISH

A sharp filleting knife with a long flexible blade is essential. You will get four fillets from a flat fish, which should be skinned before filleting. Round fish yield two fillets and are skinned after filleting.

TO FILLET FLAT FISH

1. Lay the fish on a board with its tail pointing towards you and its eyes facing up. Cut down the centre of the fish from the head to the tail along the backbone.

2. Starting at the head end, insert the blade of the knife between the flesh and the bones. Aiming to skim the blade over the bones, cut down along the flesh. When the head end of the fillet is detached, lift it and continue cutting until the whole fillet is removed.

3. Repeat this procedure to remove the second fillet.

4. Turn the fish over and cut two more fillets from the other side, to leave a clean skeleton.

TO FILLET ROUND FISH

1. Lay the fish on its side with the tail pointing towards you. Cut along the backbone from head to tail.

BONING LARGE ROUND FISH

2. Cut through behind the gills to separate the fillet from the head. Starting at the head end, insert knife between fillet and bones. Aiming to skim the knife over the bones, cut the fillet to detach completely. Holding the fish by the exposed bones, cut the remaining fillet from the ribs. Check fillets in case any bones are still attached; remove with tweezers.

1. Cut off the head and tail (or leave on if preferred). Extend the cut along the belly (used for gutting) so that it goes right to the tail.

3. Turn the fish over and repeat on the other side, working through to the backbone, being careful not to cut through the flesh.

3. To skin fillets, lay skin-side down with the tail end towards you. Make a cut at the tail end so the fillet can be lifted slightly from the skin. With salted fingers press on the exposed skin to keep it on the board. Insert the knife at a slight angle beneath the fillet and cut away from you to separate the fillet.

2. Open the fish out, then lay it on its side on a board. Carefully cut the rib bones free from the flesh on the upperside.

4. With a pair of kitchen scissors, cut through the backbone as close to the head as possible. Hold the backbone at the head end and carefully pull it free. Snip it at the tail end to remove it completely.

5. Check the flesh, removing any small bones with tweezers.

MUSSELS WITH GINGER, CHILLI AND CORIANDER

A deliciously spicy alternative to moules marinières, which uses the same method of cooking. If you prefer a creamy sauce, opt for one of the variations. Make sure you clean the mussels thoroughly, discarding any that remain open after being given a sharp tap.

SERVES 4

1 kg (2¼ lb) mussels
1 bunch of spring onions
2 garlic cloves
25 g (1 oz) piece fresh root
  ginger
1 small red chilli
15 g (½ oz) fresh coriander
  leaves
150 ml (¼ pint) white wine
40 g (1½ oz) butter
coriander sprigs, to garnish

PREPARATION TIME
20 minutes
COOKING TIME
10 minutes
FREEZING
Not suitable

175 CALS PER SERVING

1. Scrub the mussels thoroughly under cold running water, pulling away the beards from the sides of the shells. Discard mussels with damaged shells, or any that refuse to close when tapped with the back of a knife. Put the mussels in a colander and set aside.

2. Trim and shred the spring onions; peel and finely chop the garlic. Peel the ginger and chop finely or cut into fine shreds. Halve the chilli lengthways, remove the seeds, then cut into fine slivers. Strip the leaves from the coriander and set aside; reserve the stalks.

3. Put the spring onions, garlic, ginger, chilli and coriander stalks in a pan which is large enough to hold the mussels. Add the wine and 150 ml (¼ pint) water. Bring to the boil and simmer for 2 minutes.

4. Add the mussels to the pan, cover with a tight-fitting lid and cook over a moderate heat, shaking the pan occasionally, until the shells open. This will take about 4-5 minutes. Turn the mussels into a colander set over a bowl. Discard the coriander stalks and any unopened mussels.

5. Pour the liquid from the bowl back into the pan. Place over a low heat and whisk in the butter, a piece at a time. Lastly, add the coriander leaves.

6. Transfer the mussels to warmed individual serving dishes and pour over the sauce. Serve immediately, garnished with coriander sprigs.

VARIATIONS

• Stir in 60-75 ml (4-5 tbsp) crème fraîche instead of the butter.
• Replace the wine with 150 ml (¼ pint) coconut milk.

TECHNIQUE

Clean the mussels thoroughly under cold running water, removing the hairy 'beard' that protrudes from each shell.

SMOKED FISH TERRINE

This pretty terrine is perfect for entertaining, as it can be made up to 2 days in advance and stored in the refrigerator until required. I like to serve it with tiny sandwiches made from brown bread, spread with unsalted butter flavoured with a little lemon juice, and a filling of chopped fresh herbs.

SERVES 8

450 g (1 lb) smoked haddock

½ onion

1 bay leaf

few peppercorns

125 ml (4 fl oz) double cream

30 ml (2 tbsp) chopped fresh dill

5 ml (1 tsp) paprika

2.5 ml (½ tsp) cayenne pepper

30 ml (2 tbsp) lemon juice

salt and pepper

11 g (0.4 oz) packet powdered gelatine

175-225 g (6-8 oz) smoked trout, thinly sliced

75-125 g (3-4 oz) boneless smoked trout fillets

75-125 g (3-4 oz) boneless smoked mackerel fillets

CUCUMBER RELISH

½ cucumber

90 ml (3 fl oz) light olive oil

45 ml (3 tbsp) lemon juice

15 ml (1 tbsp) chopped fresh dill

PREPARATION TIME
25 minutes
COOKING TIME
15 minutes
FREEZING
Suitable

285 CALS PER SERVING

1. Put the smoked haddock in a shallow pan, and add sufficient cold water to just cover. Peel and slice the onion. Add to the pan with the bay leaf and peppercorns. Bring to the boil, lower the heat and poach gently for 15 minutes or until the fish flakes easily.

2. Remove the fish from the pan. Strain and reserve 125 ml (4 fl oz) of the poaching liquid. Flake the fish, removing any bones; leave to cool.

3. Place the flaked smoked haddock, cream, dill, paprika, cayenne and lemon juice in a food processor, and blend until smooth. Season with salt and pepper.

4. Put the reserved liquid in a small pan and sprinkle on the gelatine. Leave to soak for 5 minutes, then dissolve over a very low heat. Stir into the fish mixture.

5. Lightly oil a 900 ml (1½ pint) terrine or loaf tin and line with cling film. Line the base and sides with the smoked trout slices, reserving some for the top. Remove the skin from the trout and mackerel fillets, then halve lengthways.

6. Spoon a third of the puréed fish mixture into the bottom of the terrine and spread evenly. Lay half the trout and mackerel fillets on top, then cover with half the remaining puréed mixture. Repeat with the remaining fish fillets and puréed mixture, smoothing the surface.

Cover with the rest of the smoked trout slices. Chill in the refrigerator for at least 3 hours, until firm.

7. To make the relish, halve the cucumber lengthways and scoop out the seeds, using a teaspoon. Finely dice the cucumber flesh. Whisk together the oil and lemon juice in a bowl. Stir in the dill and diced cucumber, then season with salt and pepper.

8. To serve, turn out the terrine onto a board and remove the cling film. Cut into slices and serve with salad leaves.

VARIATIONS

Use smoked salmon rather than smoked trout to line the tin. Smoked cod can be used in place of the haddock.

TECHNIQUE

Layer the smoked fish fillets and puréed fish mixture in the lined tin, spreading evenly.

GRILLED KING PRAWNS WITH A SPICY TOMATO AND PEPPER SAUCE

This recipe is based on a classic Spanish romesco sauce, which can be served with almost any fish, hot or cold. It's a tomato-based sauce with sweet red pepper, chilli and ground toasted almonds added, to lend an interesting texture and flavour. Choose prawns of an equal size and make sure there's plenty to go round – they disappear very quickly!

SERVES 4

24 raw king prawns in shell
30-45 ml (2-3 tbsp) olive oil
SAUCE
1 onion
4 garlic cloves
1 canned pimiento, drained
2 ripe plum tomatoes
60 ml (4 tbsp) olive oil
2.5 ml (½ tsp) dried chilli flakes
75 ml (5 tbsp) fish stock
30 ml (2 tbsp) white wine
10 blanched almonds
15 ml (1 tbsp) red wine vinegar
salt
TO GARNISH
flat-leaf parsley sprigs

PREPARATION TIME
10 minutes
COOKING TIME
40 minutes
FREEZING
Not suitable

315 CALS PER SERVING

1. To make the sauce, peel and chop the onion and garlic, setting aside one of the chopped cloves. Chop the pimiento.

2. Immerse the tomatoes in a bowl of boiling water for 30 seconds, then refresh in cold water. Drain, then peel away the skins. Roughly chop the tomato flesh.

3. Heat 30 ml (2 tbsp) of the oil in a pan, add the onion and garlic, and cook gently until softened. Add the chopped tomatoes and pimiento, together with the chilli flakes, fish stock and wine. Cover and simmer for 30 minutes.

4. Preheat the grill and spread the almonds on a baking sheet. Toast the almonds under the grill until golden; alternatively dry-fry them in a pan. Transfer to a food processor or blender and grind coarsely. Add the remaining oil, the vinegar, reserved garlic and salt to taste. Work until evenly combined. Add the tomato sauce and blend until smooth.

5. Remove the heads from the prawns and, using a sharp knife, slit each one

down the back and remove the black intestinal vein. Rinse in cold water, and dry on kitchen paper.

6. Preheat the grill. Toss the prawns in olive oil, then spread out in the grill pan in an even layer. Grill for about 2-3 minutes on each side, until the shells have turned pink. Arrange on a serving platter, garnish with parsley and serve with the sauce.

NOTE: If canned pimiento is unavailable, replace with a grilled red pepper, skin removed.

TECHNIQUE

Using a small sharp knife, slit each prawn along the back and remove the dark intestinal vein.

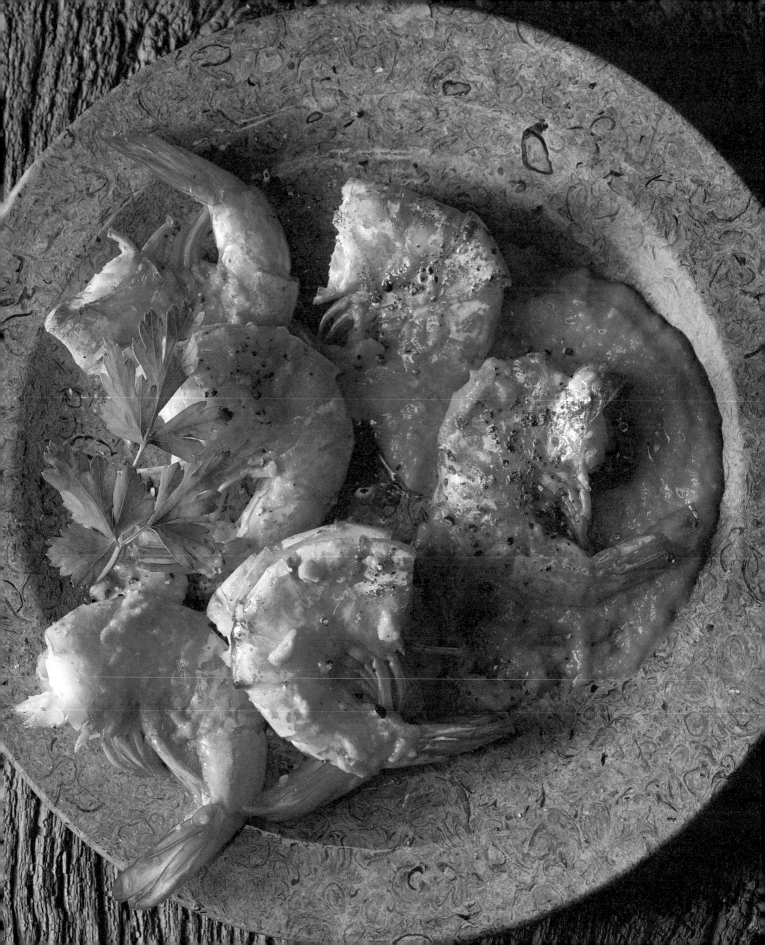

PINK TROUT WITH MUSTARD AND HERB SAUCE

Pink trout fillets are rolled and baked in a piquant marinade, flavoured with tarragon wine vinegar and pink peppercorns. The sauce is a variation of the classic gravadlax accompaniment. Serve with rye bread, and a chilled white wine.

SERVES 6

6 pink trout fillets, skinned
salt and pepper
½ small onion
150 ml (¼ pint) tarragon
  wine vinegar
15 ml (1 tbsp) pink peppercorns
25 g (1 oz) soft brown sugar
MUSTARD AND HERB
  SAUCE
15 ml (1 tbsp) wholegrain
  mustard
45 ml (3 tbsp) Dijon
  mustard
15 ml (1 tbsp) clear honey
30 ml (2 tbsp) tarragon
  wine vinegar
45 ml (3 tbsp) sunflower oil
15 ml (1 tbsp) chopped
  fresh tarragon
TO GARNISH
tarragon sprigs

PREPARATION TIME
15 minutes
COOKING TIME
35 minutes
FREEZING
Not suitable

265 CALS PER SERVING

1. Preheat the oven to 180°C (350°F) Mark 4. Lay the trout fillets, skinned-side up, on a board and season with salt and pepper. Starting at the tail end, roll each fillet up quite tightly.

2. Place the rolled fillets in a baking dish in which they fit snugly (to prevent them unrolling).

3. Peel and slice the onion. Place in a saucepan with the vinegar, peppercorns, sugar and 150 ml (¼ pint) water. Bring to the boil, then pour the hot liquid over the trout fillets. Cover the dish and bake for about 35 minutes. Leave the fish to cool in the liquid.

4. To make the mustard and herb sauce, put the mustards, honey, vinegar, oil and chopped tarragon in a bowl and whisk until evenly blended.

5. To serve, carefully remove the rolled trout fillets from the cooking liquor and transfer to a serving platter. Spoon the sauce over them and garnish with tarragon sprigs.

TECHNIQUE

Starting at the tail end, roll up each trout fillet quite tightly.

Glazed Salmon Tarts

These little tarts are filled with a creamy salmon mixture, topped with a layer of hollandaise sauce, then grilled until golden and deliciously melting. Serve them on a bed of baby spinach leaves.

SERVES 6

PASTRY

225 g (8 oz) plain flour

110 g (4 oz) butter

1 egg yolk (size 1)

15 ml (1 tbsp) chilled water

FILLING

1 shallot

25 g (1 oz) butter

25 g (1 oz) plain flour

300 ml (½ pint) milk

275 g (10 oz) cooked salmon

1 egg yolk

15 ml (1 tbsp) chopped
   fresh dill or parsley

salt and pepper

15 ml (1 tbsp) lemon juice

HOLLANDAISE SAUCE

40 ml (2½ tbsp) wine
   vinegar

3 peppercorns

1 bay leaf

1 blade of mace

1 egg yolk (size 1)

75 g (3 oz) butter

lemon juice, to taste

TO GARNISH

baby spinach leaves

dill or parsley sprigs

PREPARATION TIME

25 minutes, plus resting

COOKING TIME

30 minutes

FREEZING

Not suitable

560 CALS PER SERVING

1. To make the pastry, sift the flour into a bowl and rub in the butter until the mixture resembles fine breadcrumbs. Add the egg yolk and sufficient chilled water to mix to a smooth dough. Wrap in cling film and leave to rest in the refrigerator for 30 minutes.

2. Preheat the oven to 190°C (375°F) Mark 5. Roll out the pastry thinly on a lightly floured surface and use to line six individual 10 cm (4 inch) tart tins. Prick the bases with a fork, then line each one with a square of foil. Fill with rice or dried beans. Place on a baking sheet and bake blind for 10 minutes. Remove the foil and rice or beans.

3. Meanwhile make the filling. Peel and finely chop the shallot. Melt the butter in a pan, add the shallot and cook until softened. Add the flour and cook, stirring, for 30 seconds. Stir in the milk and slowly bring to the boil, continuing to stir, until thickened. Simmer for 2 minutes. Leave to cool.

4. Flake the cooked salmon, discarding any bones. Add the egg yolk to the sauce, then stir in the salmon and chopped dill or parsley. Season with salt, pepper and lemon juice. Divide the filling between the pastry cases and bake for 20 minutes, or until set.

5. Meanwhile make the hollandaise sauce. Put the vinegar, peppercorns, bay leaf and mace in a small pan. Bring to the boil and boil steadily to reduce to 15 ml (1 tbsp). In a small bowl, cream the egg yolk with a pinch of salt and a quarter of the butter. Place the bowl over a pan of simmering water and beat until slightly thickened. Strain in the vinegar, then beat in the remaining butter, a little at a time, until the sauce has thickened. Season with salt, pepper and lemon juice to taste.

6. Preheat the grill. Spoon the hollandaise sauce over the filling in the tarts and place under the grill for about 2 minutes to brown. If necessary, protect the pastry edges with foil to prevent over-browning. Serve warm on a bed of spinach leaves, garnished with dill or parsley sprigs.

NOTE: To save time, use ready-made hollandaise which is available in jars: you will need about 90 ml (6 tbsp).

TECHNIQUE

Line six 10 cm (4 inch) tart tins with the pastry, pressing it well into the edges. Prick the bases with a fork.

GRILLED AVOCADO STUFFED WITH CRAB

Soft goat's cheese lends a mild, fresh taste and creamy texture to the crab meat. If available, choose small Hass avocados for their nutty flavour. Serve the stuffed avocados, thickly sliced, on a bed of crisp colourful salad leaves, lightly dressed with olive oil and lemon juice.

SERVES 4

125 g (4 oz) white crab meat
125 g (4 oz) fresh soft goat's cheese
5 ml (1 tsp) chopped fresh tarragon
salt and pepper
15 ml (1 tbsp) lemon juice
2 ripe avocados
50 g (2 oz) brown crab meat
2 plum tomatoes
DRESSING
15 ml (1 tbsp) walnut oil
30 ml (2 tbsp) olive oil
15 ml (1 tbsp) lemon juice
TO SERVE
salad leaves

PREPARATION TIME
10 minutes
COOKING TIME
10 minutes
FREEZING
Not suitable

390 CALS PER SERVING

1. In a bowl, loosen the white crab meat with a fork, removing any pieces of shell. Add 50 g (2 oz) of the goat's cheese and the chopped tarragon. Mix together with a fork, seasoning with salt and pepper to taste.

2. Cut the avocados in half and remove the stones. Brush the cut surfaces with lemon juice to prevent discolouration. Divide the brown crab meat between the four avocado halves, spooning it into the cavities.

3. Divide the white crab meat mixture between the avocados, mounding it over the brown meat and spreading it over the avocado.

4. Slice the tomatoes thinly and arrange over the crab. Crumble the remaining goat's cheese on top of the tomatoes and season with pepper.

5. Preheat the grill to medium. Place the avocados on a baking sheet or in an ovenproof dish and grill for about 10 minutes, until the cheese has browned and the avocado is warm.

6. Whisk together the ingredients for the dressing in a small bowl, seasoning with salt and pepper to taste.

7. To serve, cut the avocados crosswise into thick slices and arrange on a bed of salad leaves. Drizzle with the dressing. Serve warm or cold.

TECHNIQUE

Spoon the white crab meat mixture on top of the brown meat and spread it over the avocado.

BOUILLABAISSE

The most famous of all Mediterranean fish soups, this colourful combination of fish and shellfish in a flavourful broth originated in Marseilles. Some of the fish included in the authentic version are unavailable in this country but, as you will find here, it is possible to create a delicious alternative – using varieties which can be obtained from good fishmongers. Serve with plenty of crusty bread.

SERVES 4-6

1.5 kg (3¼ lb) mixed fish
   and shellfish, such as red
   mullet, John Dory,
   monkfish, red snapper,
   whiting, large prawns,
   clams, crab claws
1 onion, peeled
1 leek
1 celery stick
225 g (8 oz) plum tomatoes
   (or other well-flavoured
   tomatoes)
pinch of saffron strands
90 ml (3 fl oz) olive oil
2 garlic cloves, crushed
1 bouquet garni
1 strip of orange peel
2.5 ml (½ tsp) fennel seeds
salt and pepper
15 ml (1 tbsp) sun-dried
   tomato paste
10 ml (2 tsp) Pernod
30-45 ml (2-3 tbsp) chopped
   parsley

PREPARATION TIME
15 minutes
COOKING TIME
About 50 minutes
FREEZING
Not suitable

515-340 CALS PER SERVING

1. Cut the heads, tails and fins off the fish and put them in a pan with 1.2 litres (2 pints) water. Bring to the boil and simmer for 15 minutes. Strain and reserve the stock.

2. Cut the fish into large chunks, but leave shellfish in their shells.

3. Slice the onion, leek and celery. Immerse the tomatoes in a bowl of boiling water for 30 seconds, then drain and refresh under cold running water. Peel away the skins. Soak the saffron strands in 15-30 ml (1-2 tbsp) boiling water.

4. Heat the oil in a large pan, add the onion, leek and celery and cook until softened. Add the tomatoes, garlic, bouquet garni, orange peel and fennel seeds. Add the saffron with its soaking liquid, and the reserved fish stock. Season with salt and pepper, bring to the boil and simmer for 30-40 minutes.

5. Add the shellfish and boil for about 6 minutes. Add the fish and cook for a further 6-8 minutes, until it flakes easily. If necessary, add a little water to ensure there is enough liquid to cover the fish.

6. Using a slotted spoon, transfer the fish to a warmed serving platter. Keep the liquid boiling, to allow the oil to emulsify with the broth. Add the sun-dried tomato paste and Pernod to the broth and check the seasoning. Serve the broth and fish separately, sprinkled with parsley.

NOTE: Croûtons can be served with the broth. To make these, fry small chunks of bread in olive oil until golden and crisp, drain well on kitchen paper, then sprinkle lightly with salt.

TECHNIQUE

For the fish stock, cut the heads, tails and fins off the fish and put them in a pan with 1.2 litres (2 pints) water.

PRAWN AND FENNEL SOUP

This is a sophisticated soup, with a delicate taste, texture and colour. The fennel lends a subtle aniseed flavour, which is heightened by the addition of a little Pernod. If possible, buy fennel with a generous amount of fronds to use as a pretty garnish.

SERVES 4

2 shallots

30 ml (2 tbsp) sunflower oil

125 g (4 oz) butter

900 g (2 lb) raw prawns in
   shell

juice of ½ lemon

45 ml (3 tbsp) Pernod

1 bay leaf

1 fresh parsley stalk

1 blade of mace

1 large fennel bulb, about
   300 g (10 oz)

1.2 litres (2 pints) fish stock

150 ml (¼ pint) white wine

40 g (1½ oz) flour

salt and white pepper

45 ml (3 tbsp) single cream

PREPARATION TIME
20 minutes
COOKING TIME
35 minutes
FREEZING
Suitable

495 CALS PER SERVING

1. Peel and chop the shallots. Heat the oil and 25 g (1 oz) butter in a large pan. Add the prawns and fry, turning them with a wooden spoon, until they are just beginning to change colour.

2. Add the shallots, lemon juice and Pernod. Continue to cook for about 2 minutes, until the prawns have turned completely pink. Remove from the heat and leave to cool.

3. Remove the prawns from the pan with a slotted spoon, reserving the shallots and liquid. Carefully shell the prawns, reserving the shells, and set aside.

4. Put the prawn shells in a large saucepan with the bay leaf, parsley and mace. Slice the fennel, reserving the fronds, and add to the pan. Pour in the fish stock and white wine. Bring to the boil, lower the heat, cover and simmer for about 30 minutes. Strain the stock and set aside.

5. Place the prawns in a food processor with 40 g (1½ oz) of the butter, then blend to a paste.

6. Melt the remaining 40 g (1½ oz) butter in a large pan, add the flour and cook, stirring, for 30 seconds. Gradually stir in the stock. Slowly bring to the boil, stirring, then simmer for 2 minutes. Add the reserved shallots and liquid, together with the prawn paste. Whisk until thoroughly combined. Season with salt and pepper to taste.

7. Ladle into warmed soup bowls and swirl in the cream. Serve garnished with fennel fronds.

NOTE: For a smoother, velvety texture, blend in an electric blender (which works better for soups than a food processor), or pass through a sieve, at the end of stage 6. Reheat gently before serving.

VARIATION

If raw prawns are unavailable, use 450 g (1 lb) cooked shelled ones instead, simply adding them at stage 5. Use a well-flavoured fish stock (to compensate for the lack of prawn shells).

TECHNIQUE

Purée the shelled prawns with 40 g (1½ oz) of the butter to a smooth paste.

SMOKED HADDOCK CHOWDER

This hearty soup is perfect winter fare. Served with crusty bread and some good mature Cheddar cheese, it is sustaining enough to serve as a complete meal. Undyed smoked haddock is now widely available as an alternative to the familiar vibrant yellow dyed version.

SERVES 6

700 g (1½ lb) smoked
  haddock
900 ml (1½ pints) milk
4 rashers back bacon,
  derinded
1 small onion
675 g (1½ lb) potatoes
450 ml (¾ pint) fish stock
200 g (7 oz) canned
  sweetcorn
60 ml (4 tbsp) double cream
25 g (1 oz) butter
salt and pepper
paprika, to taste

PREPARATION TIME
15 minutes
COOKING TIME
20-25 minutes
FREEZING
Not suitable

415 CALS PER SERVING

1. Put the fish in a saucepan with half of the milk. Slowly bring to the boil, then simmer, covered, for about 10 minutes until just cooked. Lift the fish out onto a plate with a slotted spoon and leave to cool. Reserve the milk.

2. Roughly chop the bacon. Place in a non-stick frying pan and fry gently until the fat runs out, but don't let the bacon become crisp.

3. Peel and chop the onion. Peel the potatoes and cut into even-sized cubes.

4. Remove the skin and bones from the fish and flake into largish pieces.

5. Put the fish in a large saucepan with the fish stock, bacon, onion, potatoes and sweetcorn. Strain in the reserved milk from cooking the fish. Add the remaining milk and bring to the boil. Lower the heat and simmer for 10-15 minutes, until the potatoes are cooked, but not mushy.

6. Stir in the cream and butter. Season with salt, pepper and paprika to taste. Serve piping hot, with crusty bread.

NOTE: Some supermarkets now sell 'lardons', or chunky little bacon dice. These are perfect for this soup.

TECHNIQUE

Using two forks, flake the cooked smoked haddock into fairly large pieces.

PRAWNS AND CUCUMBER IN A SPICY SAUCE

This is quite an unusual dish, as it includes cooked cucumber, an ingredient you normally expect to find raw in a salad. Here the refreshing coolness of the cucumber contrasts perfectly with the spices and fresh chillies. Serve with basmati or Thai fragrant rice, or warm pitta bread or chappatis if you prefer.

SERVES 4

2 medium cucumbers
salt
2 onions
2 garlic cloves
50 g (2 oz) butter
20 ml (4 tsp) plain flour
10 ml (2 tsp) turmeric
5 ml (1 tsp) ground
   cinnamon
10 ml (2 tsp) sugar
1.25 ml (¼ tsp) ground
   cloves
750 ml (1¼ pints) coconut
   milk
300 ml (½ pint) fish stock
15 g (½ oz) fresh root
   ginger
3-4 green chillies
450 g (1 lb) raw tiger
   prawns (in shells)
juice of 1 lime
30 ml (2 tbsp) chopped
   fresh coriander
TO GARNISH
coriander sprigs

PREPARATION TIME
20 minutes, plus standing
COOKING TIME
30 minutes
FREEZING Not suitable

450 CALS PER SERVING

1. Cut the cucumbers in half lengthways and remove the seeds, using a teaspoon. Cut into 2.5 cm (1 inch) chunks. Place the cucumber in a colander set over a bowl and sprinkle with salt. Leave for 30 minutes, to allow the salt to extract the excess juices.

2. Peel and slice the onions; peel and chop the garlic. Melt the butter in a pan, add the onions and garlic and cook for about 5 minutes, until softened. Add the flour, turmeric, cinnamon, 5 ml (1 tsp) salt, the sugar and cloves; cook, stirring, for 2 minutes. Add the coconut milk and fish stock, bring to the boil and simmer for 5 minutes.

3. Meanwhile, rinse the cucumber thoroughly under cold running water to remove the salt. Peel the ginger and cut into very thin slices. Halve the chillies, remove the seeds and slice thinly.

4. Add the ginger, chillies and cucumber to the sauce, and continue to cook for a further 10 minutes.

5. Meanwhile, shell the prawns, leaving on the tail shells if preferred. Split each one down the back and remove the black intestinal vein. Add the prawns to the sauce and cook for a further 5-6 minutes until they turn pink.

6. Just before serving, stir in the lime juice and chopped coriander. Garnish with sprigs of coriander, and whole green chillies if desired.

NOTE: If raw prawns are difficult to come by, use cooked ones instead. Add them to the sauce and heat through for 2-3 minutes — no longer or they will become rubbery.

TECHNIQUE

Carefully peel away the shells from the prawns, leaving on the pretty tail shells if preferred.

GRILLED SCALLOPS IN BASIL LEAVES

Tender fresh scallops are wrapped in fresh basil leaves, then in strips of grilled red and yellow peppers, and threaded onto skewers with chunks of courgette. When grilled the scallops remain moist, protected from the fierce heat by their colourful coats! Choose scallops of a uniform size, each with the coral still attached if possible. Serve the skewers on a bed of couscous or rice.

SERVES 4

2 red peppers
2 yellow peppers
16 large fresh scallops,
    shelled (see page 5)
60 ml (4 tbsp) olive oil
salt and pepper
3 courgettes
16 large basil leaves
TO SERVE
lemon wedges

PREPARATION TIME
15 minutes
COOKING TIME
15 minutes
FREEZING
Not suitable

300 CALS PER SERVING

1. Cut the peppers into quarters, and remove the core and seeds. Preheat the grill. Place the peppers, skin-side up, on the grill rack and cook until the skins are charred and blackened. Transfer them to a bowl, cover with a plate and leave for 5 minutes; the steam created will help to loosen the skins. When the peppers are cool enough to handle, peel away the skins.

2. Place the scallops in a bowl, add 30 ml (2 tbsp) of the olive oil and season with salt and pepper. Toss the scallops to coat with the oil.

3. Cut the courgettes into chunks. Blanch in boiling water for 3 minutes. Drain thoroughly.

4. Wrap each scallop in a basil leaf, then in a piece of grilled pepper. Thread the scallops, alternately with the courgettes, onto 8 metal or wooden skewers. Brush with the remaining olive oil, and season with salt and pepper.

5. Preheat the grill and place the scallop and courgette skewers on the grill rack. Grill for about 8 minutes, turning the skewers occasionally and basting with any oil and juice in the pan. Serve immediately, with lemon wedges.

NOTE: If using wooden skewers, soak them in cold water for 20 minutes before threading on the ingredients. This prevents them from charring quickly under the grill.

VARIATION

Cook the skewers on a barbecue. Lay some herb sprigs on the grid to impart flavour and aroma.

TECHNIQUE

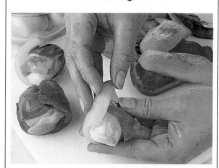

Wrap each scallop in a basil leaf, then a grilled pepper quarter.

LOBSTER WITH BASIL MAYONNAISE

Lobster is best served in a simple manner – the firm, juicy, subtle-flavoured flesh enhanced with a good mayonnaise, or served hot with a butter sauce. This recipe relies on the former, with the addition of fresh basil, and a lightly cooked compote of plum tomatoes, spiked with balsamic vinegar.

SERVES 4

4 cooked lobsters, each about 450 g (1 lb)
BASIL MAYONNAISE
2 egg yolks
5 ml (1 tsp) Dijon mustard
30 ml (2 tbsp) lemon juice
salt and pepper
125 ml (4 fl oz) olive oil
125 ml (4 fl oz) sunflower or groundnut oil
25 g (1 oz) chopped fresh basil
TOMATO COMPOTE
1 shallot
30 ml (2 tbsp) olive oil
350 g (12 oz) plum tomatoes
15 ml (1 tbsp) sugar
10 ml (2 tsp) balsamic vinegar
TO SERVE
50 g (2 oz) rocket leaves

PREPARATION TIME
30 minutes
COOKING TIME
8 minutes
FREEZING
Not suitable

550 CALS PER SERVING

1. First prepare the mayonnaise. Place the egg yolks in a small bowl, and add the mustard, 15 ml (1 tbsp) of the lemon juice and a little salt and pepper. Beat until thoroughly combined. Continue beating, while adding the oils (mixed together), drop by drop. The mayonnaise should start to thicken gradually. Once it begins to thicken add the oil in a thin continuous stream, beating constantly. When the mixture is thick and smooth, add the remaining lemon juice, check the seasoning and stir in the basil. Cover and refrigerate.

2. To make the tomato compote, peel and finely chop the shallot. Heat the oil in a pan, add the shallot and cook gently until softened. Meanwhile, immerse the tomatoes in a bowl of boiling water for 30 seconds. Refresh under cold water, peel away the skins, then chop into rough chunks. Add to the shallot, with the sugar and vinegar. Stir well, increase the heat and cook for 3 minutes. Using a slotted spoon, transfer the tomatoes to a bowl and continue cooking the liquid until reduced and slightly syrupy; add to the tomatoes. Season with salt and pepper to taste and leave to cool.

3. Split the lobsters in half and prepare according to the step-by-step instructions on page 7. Reserve the smaller claws (and legs if you wish) for the garnish. Cut the tail meat into thick slices.

4. Arrange the lobster and rocket leaves on individual serving plates, placing the claws and legs to one side. Place a spoonful of the mayonnaise and a spoonful of tomato compote on each plate. Equip everyone with a lobster pick or fine metal skewer, to extract the meat from the legs.

NOTE: Use 300 ml (½ pint) quality ready-made mayonnaise for convenience if you prefer; flavour it with basil.

The calorie count assumes that approximately half of the mayonnaise will be eaten with the lobster.

TECHNIQUE

Lay the lobsters, back upwards, on a board. Using a sharp knife, split the lobster lengthwise cleanly in two, piercing the cross at the centre of the head.

PAN-FRIED RED MULLET WITH CITRUS AND BASIL

Red mullet – with its attractive pink skin – is certainly one of the prettiest fish, and has an excellent flavour. As it is quite a bony fish, most people prefer to eat it filleted – a helpful fishmonger should oblige with this fiddly task. I like to serve this light dish with steamed couscous and a leafy salad.

SERVES 4

4 red mullet, each about
   225 g (8 oz), filleted
90 ml (6 tbsp) olive oil
10 peppercorns, crushed
2 oranges
1 lemon
salt and pepper
30 ml (2 tbsp) plain flour
15 g (½ oz) butter
2 anchovies
15 g (½ oz) shredded fresh
   basil

PREPARATION TIME
10 minutes, plus marinating
COOKING TIME
10 minutes
FREEZING
Not suitable

430 CALS PER SERVING

1. Place the fish fillets in a shallow dish, in a single layer. Drizzle over the olive oil and sprinkle with the peppercorns. Peel one of the oranges, removing all of the skin and white pith, then cut into thin slices. Lay the orange slices over the fish. Cover and leave to marinate in the refrigerator for 4 hours.

2. Halve the lemon. Remove the skin and white pith from one half, then slice thinly. Squeeze the juice from the other half and reserve.

3. Using a fish slice lift the fish out of the marinade, reserving the marinade, and pat dry on kitchen paper. Season with salt and pepper, then dust lightly with flour.

4. Heat 45 ml (3 tbsp) of the marinade in a sauté pan or frying pan. Add the red mullet fillets and fry for 2 minutes on each side. Remove from the pan and set aside; keep warm. Discard the oil remaining in the pan.

5. Melt the butter in the pan with the remaining marinade. Add the anchovies and crush until dissolved. Add the juice of the remaining orange and the reserved lemon juice. Season and cook until slightly reduced. Lastly, stir in the shredded basil.

6. Pour the citrus sauce over the fish and garnish with the orange and lemon slices. Serve at once.

VARIATION

If red mullet is unavailable, use sole fillets instead.

TECHNIQUE

Lay the red mullet fillets in a shallow dish, in a single layer. Drizzle over the olive oil, then sprinkle with the peppercorns.

FRIED SKATE WINGS WITH OLIVE AND HERB SAUCE

Skate wings have a wonderful texture and are surprisingly easy to eat, as the flesh just falls away from the bones. This is a relatively quick and easy dish, although you may need two frying pans to cook the fish. Serve with boiled new potatoes and lightly cooked fresh spinach.

SERVES 4

4 skate wings, each
   300-350 g (10-12 oz)
salt and pepper
60 ml (4 tbsp) plain flour
50 g (2 oz) butter
30 ml (2 tbsp) oil
SAUCE
2 garlic cloves
8 anchovy fillets
30 ml (2 tbsp) capers,
   drained and rinsed
10 ml (2 tsp) black olive
   paste
15 ml (1 tbsp) sun-dried
   tomato paste
60 ml (4 tbsp) chopped
   fresh parsley
15 ml (1 tbsp) chopped
   fresh chives
60 ml (4 tbsp) extra-virgin
   olive oil
juice of 1 lemon
TO GARNISH
few chives

PREPARATION TIME
10 minutes
COOKING TIME
12 minutes
FREEZING
Not suitable

600 CALS PER SERVING

1. First make the sauce. Crush the garlic cloves and place in a bowl. Drain the anchovy fillets on kitchen paper, chop finely and add to the garlic. Add the capers, olive paste, sun-dried tomato paste, parsley, chives, olive oil and lemon juice. Mix thoroughly.

2. If the skate wings are very large, cut them into more manageable pieces. Season with salt and pepper and dust with flour.

3. Heat the butter and oil in a very large frying pan, or two smaller ones. When the butter begins to foam, add the skate wings and fry gently for about 5 minutes on each side or until just cooked. To test, prise a little of the flesh away from the bone with the tip of a knife: if it comes away easily the fish is cooked.

4. Pour the sauce around the fish and heat through for 1-2 minutes. Serve immediately, garnished with chives.

NOTE: Both olive and sun-dried tomato pastes are available from larger supermarkets and good delicatessens. If unavailable, or if you prefer a coarse textured sauce, use chopped pitted olives and sun-dried tomatoes instead.

TECHNIQUE

To check if the fish is cooked, prise a little of the flesh away from the bone with the tip of a knife. If it comes away easily the skate is cooked.

TURBOT WITH MUSHROOMS, BABY ONIONS AND POTATOES

As turbot is rather an expensive fish it is usually reserved for special occasions. However this recipe also works well with cod and haddock (see variation). Shiitake mushrooms add a meaty taste and texture to the dish. Choose the smallest onions and new potatoes of an even size.

SERVES 4

12 baby onions

20 small new potatoes

150 g (5 oz) butter

90 ml (3 fl oz) olive oil

salt and pepper

225 g (8 oz) shiitake
    mushrooms

600 ml (1 pint) chicken
    stock

60 ml (4 tbsp) chopped
    fresh parsley

4 turbot steaks, each about
    175 g (6 oz)

PREPARATION TIME
15 minutes
COOKING TIME
20 minutes
FREEZING
Not suitable

875 CALS PER SERVING

1. Blanch the baby onions in a pan of boiling water for 5 minutes, then drain and plunge into cold water. Remove and peel away the skins. Trim off the root ends. Scrub the new potatoes.

2. Heat 50 g (2 oz) of the butter in a large sauté pan. Add 30 ml (2 tbsp) olive oil. When hot, add the onions and potatoes and cook slowly for about 10 minutes until golden. Lower the heat, season with salt and pepper and cook for a further 10 minutes.

3. In another pan, heat 25 g (1 oz) butter with 15 ml (1 tbsp) olive oil. When the butter starts to foam, add the mushrooms and cook for 2 minutes. Add the chicken stock, bring to the boil and simmer for 5 minutes. Remove the mushrooms from the stock with a slotted spoon, and add to the onions and potatoes. Boil the stock rapidly over a high heat until reduced by about half.

4. Stir the parsley into the mushroom, potato and onion mixture, then transfer to a warmed serving dish. Keep warm.

5. Add the remaining oil to the sauté pan (that the onions and potatoes were cooked in). Add the turbot steaks and cook for about 4 minutes on each side, depending on their thickness, until browned and cooked through (see technique). Remove from the pan, and arrange on top of the vegetables.

6. Meanwhile, whisk remaining butter into the reduced stock, bit by bit, until it forms a smooth, glossy sauce. Spoon over the fish and serve immediately.

VARIATION

Replace the turbot with cod steaks or thick pieces of haddock fillet.

TECHNIQUE

To test whether the fish is cooked, prise the flesh slightly away from the bone. If it comes away easily, the fish is cooked.

NAVARIN OF MONKFISH

This is a pretty, delicate-tasting fish stew. Monkfish has a good firm texture and holds its shape when cooked in large chunks. Baby carrots, asparagus tips and broad beans are chosen for their fresh taste and colour. Both fish and vegetables are cooked in wine and fish stock, which is enhanced with cream, lemon and subtle-tasting chervil to serve. Buttered baby new potatoes are the perfect accompaniment.

SERVES 4-6

1 kg (2¼ lb) monkfish
225 g (8 oz) baby carrots
175 g (6 oz) shelled fresh or
  frozen broad beans
225 g (8 oz) asparagus tips
1 onion
1 garlic clove
25 g (1 oz) butter
30 ml (2 tbsp) sunflower oil
salt and pepper
60 ml (4 tbsp) plain flour
150 ml (¼ pint) dry white
  wine
300 ml (½ pint) fish stock
  (see right)
15 ml (1 tbsp) lemon juice
45 ml (3 tbsp) double cream
30 ml (2 tbsp) chopped
  fresh chervil
chervil sprigs, to garnish

PREPARATION TIME
15-25 minutes
COOKING TIME
25 minutes
FREEZING
Not suitable

445-300 CALS PER SERVING

1. Fillet the monkfish by cutting down either side of the central bone. Remove any membrane and cut the fish into large chunks. (Reserve the bone and trimmings for the stock.)

2. Scrub the carrots if necessary, and trim. Slip the broad beans out of their skins if preferred. Trim the asparagus if necessary. Peel and slice the onion; crush the garlic.

3. Melt half the butter and oil in a deep sauté pan. Add the carrots, asparagus, onion and garlic, and cook gently until just beginning to brown. Remove from the pan and set aside.

4. Season the fish with salt and pepper, and lightly dust with flour. Melt the remaining butter and oil in the pan, add the fish and brown on all sides. Remove from the pan and set aside.

5. Add the wine to the hot pan, scraping up any residue from the bottom. Simmer for 2 minutes, then return the vegetables and fish to the pan.

6. Add the broad beans, then pour in the fish stock. Bring to the boil, cover and simmer gently for about 15 minutes, until the fish is cooked.

7. Stir in the lemon juice, cream and chervil. Serve garnished with chervil sprigs.

FISH STOCK

Use the bone and any trimmings from the fish to make the stock. Place in a saucepan and add enough water to cover. Add a slice of onion, a bay leaf, some peppercorns and a few sprigs of chervil or parsley. Bring to the boil, cover and simmer for 20 minutes.

TECHNIQUE

Season the fish with salt and pepper, then lightly dust with flour.

BRAISED MONKFISH WRAPPED IN PARMA HAM WITH PUY LENTILS

Monkfish is a firm-fleshed fish, which can withstand cooking methods that are more suited to meat. Here the fish is wrapped in delicate thin slices of Parma ham, pan-fried until golden, and then gently braised on a bed of Puy lentils.

SERVES 4-6

1 kg (2¼ lb) monkfish tail
  (whole)
1 small lemon
15 ml (1 tbsp) chopped
  fresh marjoram
salt and pepper
4-6 thin slices Parma ham
1 small onion
1 carrot
1 celery stick
1 garlic clove
45 ml (3 tbsp) olive oil
350 g (12 oz) Puy lentils
150 ml (¼ pint) red wine
30 ml (2 tbsp) chopped
  fresh coriander or parsley

PREPARATION TIME
15 minutes, plus marinating
COOKING TIME
40 minutes
FREEZING
Not suitable

550-365 CALS PER SERVING

1. Fillet the monkfish by cutting down either side of the central bone. Peel the lemon, removing all the white pith, then cut into thin slices. Lay the fish cut-side up on a board and sprinkle with the marjoram. Season with salt and pepper. Lay the lemon slices over one piece of fish, then sandwich together with the other monkfish fillet.

2. Wrap the fish in the Parma ham, making sure that it is completely covered. Tie at 5 cm (2 inch) intervals with fine string. Cover and leave in a cool place for 1-2 hours to allow the flavours to develop.

3. Peel the onion and carrot. Finely dice the onion, carrot and celery. Peel and finely chop the garlic. Heat 30 ml (2 tbsp) olive oil in a saucepan, add the garlic and vegetables and cook, stirring, for about 8 minutes until golden. Stir in the lentils and wine. Add sufficient water to cover, bring to the boil and cook for 10 minutes.

4. Heat the remaining oil in a large frying pan. Add the monkfish parcel and fry, turning, until the Parma ham is browned all over. Carefully remove the fish parcel

and transfer the lentils to the frying pan. Replace the fish on top, burying it into the lentils slightly. Cover the pan and cook over a medium-low heat for about 20 minutes, until the lentils are cooked and the juices from the fish run clear, when tested with a knife.

5. Remove the string from the fish, then cut into thick slices. Serve on a bed of lentils, sprinkled with the chopped coriander or parsley.

TECHNIQUE

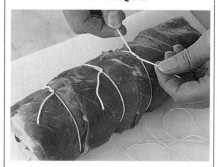

Wrap the monkfish parcel in the Parma ham to cover completely, then tie at 5 cm (2 inch) intervals with cotton string.

SALMON EN PAPILLOTE WITH LIME BUTTER SAUCE

Salmon steaks – scented with lime and ginger – are gently cooked in paper parcels, then served with a rich butter sauce flavoured with lime and dry sherry. The sauce can be made in advance and gently reheated in a bain-marie as the fish is cooking, making this recipe a perfect dinner party dish.

SERVES 4

75 g (3 oz) unsalted butter

2 limes

15 g (½ oz) fresh root
   ginger

4 salmon steaks, each about
   175 g (6 oz)

salt and pepper

4 spring onions, trimmed

pinch of sugar

45 ml (3 tbsp) dry sherry
   (preferably Manzanilla)

45 ml (3 tbsp) double cream

PREPARATION TIME
20 minutes
COOKING TIME
12-15 minutes
FREEZING
Not suitable

635 CALS PER SERVING

1. Preheat the oven to 200°C (400°F) Mark 6. Cut 4 baking parchment or greaseproof paper rectangles, measuring 30 x 20 cm (12 x 8 inches). Using 25 g (1 oz) of the butter, grease the paper.

2. Grate the rind from 1 lime and squeeze the juice. Peel the ginger, then cut into very fine slices or julienne strips.

3. Place a salmon steak on one half of each paper rectangle. Season with salt and pepper. Scatter the lime rind and ginger on top, then sprinkle with the lime juice. Fold the other half of the paper over the top, brushing the edges together. Make small overlapping folds along the edges to seal. Place on a baking sheet and set aside.

4. To make the sauce, chop the spring onions. Heat 15 g (½ oz) butter in a small pan, add the spring onions and cook until softened. Squeeze the juice from the remaining lime. Add to the onions with the sugar and sherry. Increase the heat and boil steadily until the liquid is reduced by half.

5. Place the fish papillotes in the oven and cook for 12-15 minutes; the parcels will puff up.

6. Add the cream to the sauce and allow to bubble for a few seconds. Gradually whisk in the remaining butter, a piece at a time, taking the pan off the heat occasionally to prevent the sauce from splitting. The sauce should be smooth and slightly thickened. Season with salt and pepper.

7. Serve the papillotes at the table, allowing each person to enjoy the fragrance as they open their own parcel. Serve the sauce separately.

NOTE: Manzanilla sherry has a dry, almost salty tang which complements the fish well. If unavailable, fino sherry could be used instead.

TECHNIQUE

Fold the paper to enclose the salmon steak, bringing the edges together, then seal.

FISH STEW WITH ARTICHOKES AND OYSTER MUSHROOMS

Chunky pieces of haddock, tender artichoke hearts and subtle-tasting oyster mushrooms are cooked together in a white wine sauce, flavoured with lemon. Serve this special occasion fish stew with mixed wild and long-grain rice, or boiled new potatoes.

SERVES 4-6

1 kg (2¼ lb) thick-cut skin-less haddock fillet

salt and pepper

45-60 ml (3-4 tbsp) plain flour

2 onions

2 garlic cloves

30 ml (2 tbsp) olive oil

25 g (1 oz) butter

300 ml (½ pint) white wine

175 ml (6 fl oz) fish stock

225 g (8 oz) oyster mushrooms

1 bay leaf

30 ml (2 tbsp) chopped fresh parsley

12 artichoke hearts in oil

1 lemon

30 ml (2 tbsp) chopped fresh basil

TO GARNISH

basil leaves

PREPARATION TIME
15 minutes
COOKING TIME
About 25 minutes
FREEZING
Not suitable

425-285 CALS PER SERVING

1. Cut the haddock into 5 cm (2 inch) pieces, removing any bones. Season with salt and pepper, and dust with flour.

2. Peel the onions and cut each one into eight wedges, retaining the root to hold the layers together. Peel and chop the garlic.

3. Heat the oil and butter in a deep sauté pan. When foaming, add the fish and cook until browned all over. Remove the fish with a slotted spoon and set aside.

4. Add the onions to the pan and cook until browned and softened. Add the garlic and cook for 2 minutes. Stir in the wine and stock, the mushrooms, bay leaf and parsley. Bring to the boil and simmer for 5 minutes.

5. Drain and halve the artichoke hearts. Cut the lemon into thin slices. Add the fish and artichokes to the sauce, then lay the lemon slices on top. Cover and cook for 10-15 minutes. Stir in the chopped basil. Serve immediately, garnished with basil leaves.

VARIATION

Use cod in place of haddock, and replace the oyster mushrooms with brown cap or open cup mushrooms.

TECHNIQUE

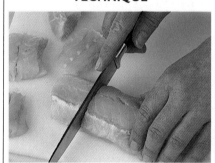

Cut the haddock fillet into 5 cm (2 inch) pieces, making sure that all bones have been removed.

SALMON AND LEEK JALOUSIE

Tender salmon fillet is encased in a rich mixture of buttery leeks, mushrooms, herbs and crème fraîche, then wrapped in puff pastry. The top of the pie is cut to resemble a Venetian blind, or *jalousie* in French. Serve the pie hot or cold, with a salad or simple accompaniment, such as new potatoes.

SERVES 4

350 g (12 oz) ready-made puff pastry (fresh or frozen and thawed)

3 leeks

40 g (1½ oz) butter

125 g (4 oz) brown cap mushrooms

1 garlic clove

15 ml (1 tbsp) chopped fresh dill

5 ml (1 tsp) chopped fresh tarragon

50 g (2 oz) fresh bread-crumbs

50 g (2 oz) Cheddar cheese

90 ml (3 fl oz) crème fraîche

salt and pepper

450 g (1 lb) piece skinless salmon fillet

1 egg, beaten

PREPARATION TIME
25 minutes
COOKING TIME
35-40 minutes
FREEZING
Suitable: Uncooked, stage 7

820 CALS PER SERVING

1. Preheat the oven to 230°C (450°F) Mark 8. Divide the pastry into two pieces, one slightly larger than the other. Roll out the larger piece on a lightly floured surface to a rectangle, measuring 30 x 23 cm (12 x 9 inches). Loosely fold in four, wrap in cling film and store in the refrigerator.

2. Roll out the smaller piece of pastry to a rectangle, measuring 25 x 18 cm (10 x 7 inches). Place on a dampened baking sheet and prick all over with a fork. Chill in refrigerator for 10 minutes, then bake for 10 minutes until crisp.

3. Thoroughly clean the leeks, then chop finely. Melt the butter in a pan, add the leeks and cook gently until soft but not coloured. Meanwhile, roughly chop the mushrooms.

4. Add the chopped mushrooms to the leeks with the garlic. Cook for 3 minutes, then remove from the heat and add the dill, tarragon, breadcrumbs, cheese and crème fraîche. Season with salt and pepper to taste.

5. Spread half the leek mixture on the cooked pastry, to the same dimensions as the salmon fillet. Lay the salmon on top, then spread the remaining leek mixture over the salmon.

6. Unfold the remaining pastry, lightly dust with flour and fold in half lengthways. Using a sharp knife, cut through the folded side at 5 mm (¼ inch) intervals, leaving a 5 cm (2 inch) border all the way round. Open out the rectangle.

7. Brush the edges of the cooked pastry with a little beaten egg, then lay the cut pastry rectangle on top. Press the edges together to seal, then press a fork around the edges to decorate.

8. Brush the jalousie with beaten egg, and bake for 10 minutes. Lower the oven temperature to 200°C (400°F) Mark 6 and bake for a further 15-20 minutes, until golden brown and crisp. Serve cut into thick slices.

TECHNIQUE

Cut through the folded side of the pastry at 5 mm (¼ inch) intervals, leaving a clear border all the way round.

PEPPERED SALMON STEAKS

Here is a variation on the classic *steak au poivre*, using salmon and a mixture of peppercorns – black, white, pink and green. It's a very quick dish, equally suitable for a dinner party or a simple supper. The spicy bite and crunchy texture of the peppercorns contrast perfectly with tender salmon.

SERVES 4

30-45 ml (2-3 tbsp) mixed
    peppercorns (see note)
4 salmon steaks, each about
    175 g (6 oz)
25 g (1 oz) butter
15 ml (1 tbsp) oil
60 ml (4 tbsp) red wine
salt
150 ml (¼ pint) crème
    fraîche
TO GARNISH
flat-leaf parsley sprigs

PREPARATION TIME
10 minutes
COOKING TIME
6-10 minutes
FREEZING
Not suitable

545 CALS PER SERVING

1. Crush the peppercorns coarsely, using a pestle and mortar or coarse grinder. Sprinkle the peppercorns onto a plate. Press the salmon steaks onto the peppercorns on both sides, so that the salmon flesh becomes encrusted with the pepper.

2. Heat the butter and oil in a large frying pan and, when the butter starts to foam, add the salmon steaks. Cook over a medium heat for about 4 minutes on each side.

3. Remove the fish from the pan using a fish slice and keep warm. Add the red wine to the pan. Increase the heat and boil steadily to reduce by about half, scraping the bottom of the pan to loosen any bits of pepper. Season with salt to taste. Add the crème fraîche and allow to bubble for a few seconds. Pour this sauce over the salmon steaks and serve immediately, garnished with flat-leaf parsley.

NOTE: Jars of mixed peppercorns are readily available from delicatessens and larger supermarkets.

VARIATION

Salmon fillets are a good substitute for those who don't like bones!

TECHNIQUE

Press both sides of the salmon steaks onto the crushed peppercorns to coat evenly.

SOLE FLORENTINE

Rolled sole fillets are baked on layers of fresh tomatoes, garlic and fresh spinach, beneath a creamy cheese sauce. This is another perfect supper dish, which can be prepared in advance. Ring the changes with other varieties of fish – cod, haddock or any other white fish would do. Serve with sauté potatoes – the other vegetables are already there!

SERVES 4

6 ripe tomatoes
25 g (1 oz) butter
1 garlic clove, crushed
1 kg (2¼ lb) fresh spinach
salt and pepper
pinch of freshly grated
  nutmeg
8 single sole fillets
CHEESE SAUCE
20 g (¾ oz) butter
20 g (¾ oz) plain flour
300 ml (½ pint) milk
50 g (2 oz) Gruyère cheese,
  grated
TOPPING
15 ml (1 tbsp) dried breadcrumbs
15 ml (1 tbsp) freshly grated
  Parmesan cheese

PREPARATION TIME
30 minutes
COOKING TIME
10-15 minutes
FREEZING
Not suitable

385 CALS PER SERVING

1. First make the cheese sauce. Melt the butter in a saucepan and stir in the flour. Cook, stirring, for 1 minute. Remove from the heat and gradually stir in the milk. Return to the heat and bring to the boil, stirring. Simmer for 2 minutes. Remove from the heat, add the cheese and mix until smooth. Season with salt and pepper. Cover the surface with a buttered piece of greaseproof paper to prevent a skin forming.

2. Preheat the oven to 180°C (350°F) Mark 4. Plunge the tomatoes into a bowl of boiling water for 30 seconds, refresh in cold water, then peel away the skins. Thickly slice the tomatoes. Melt 15 g (½ oz) butter in a frying pan and add the garlic. Add the tomatoes and fry briefly; don't let them become too soft. Transfer to a buttered ovenproof dish.

3. Clean the spinach thoroughly and remove any tough stalks. Place in a large saucepan with just the water clinging to the leaves after washing. Cover and cook for 5 minutes, shaking the pan. (You may need to cook it in two batches.) Drain the spinach well, squeezing out as much moisture as possible. Chop roughly, then return to the pan with the remaining 15 g (½ oz) butter. Season with salt, pepper and nutmeg. Cook, stirring, for 1 minute. Spread the spinach over the tomatoes.

4. Lay the sole fillets on a board, skinned-side up, and season with salt and pepper. Roll up from the tail end, then place on top of the spinach.

5. Reheat the cheese sauce and pour evenly over the fish and spinach. Sprinkle with the breadcrumbs and Parmesan and bake for 10-15 minutes until hot and bubbling. Meanwhile, preheat the grill. When the fish is cooked, place the dish under the grill to brown the topping.

NOTE: Frozen spinach can be used in place of fresh, although the colour and texture won't be quite as good.

TECHNIQUE

Drain the spinach in a sieve, pressing out as much liquid as possible with the back of a wooden spoon.

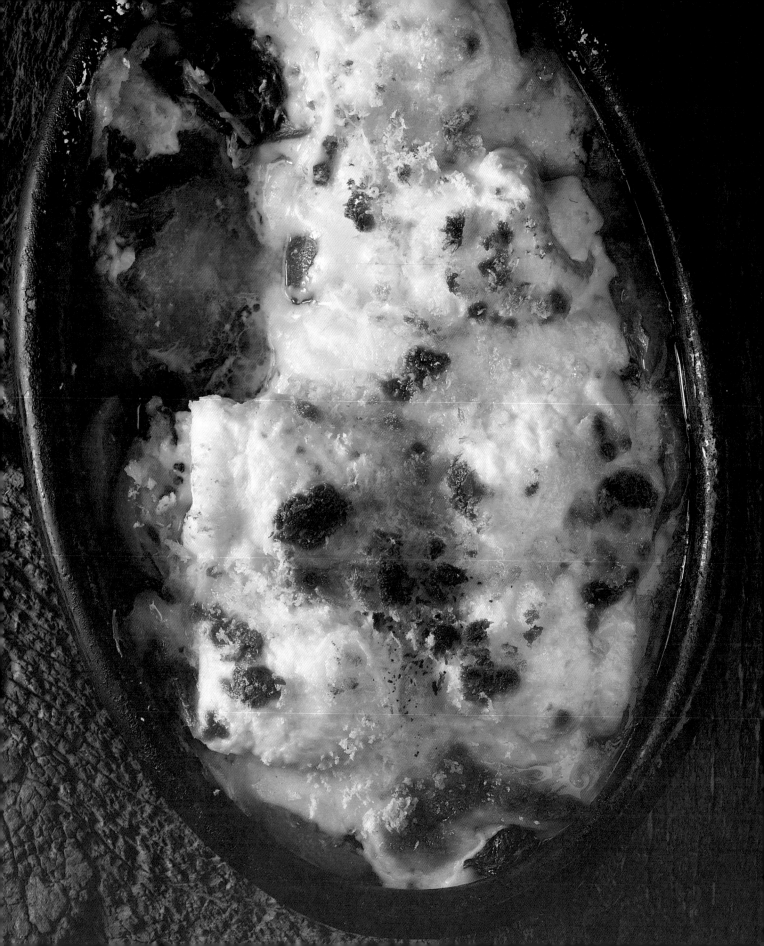

BAKED HERRING WITH AN OATMEAL, MUSHROOM AND PARSLEY STUFFING

Fresh herring are delicious pan-fried in oatmeal, or, as in this recipe, baked with an oatmeal stuffing. Oatmeal has a perfect affinity with herring, the nutty taste and texture contrasting with the oiliness of the fish. Serve the herring with boiled new potatoes and a green vegetable, such as broccoli or courgettes.

SERVES 4

1 small onion
15 ml (1 tbsp) sunflower oil
125 g (4 oz) brown cap
   mushrooms
30 ml (2 tbsp) oatmeal
45 ml (3 tbsp) chopped
   fresh parsley
juice of ½ lemon
salt and pepper
1 egg yolk
25 g (1 oz) butter
4 herrings, each about 300 g
   (10 oz), cleaned
TO SERVE
lemon wedges

PREPARATION TIME
20 minutes
COOKING TIME
15-20 minutes
FREEZING
Not suitable

500 CALS PER SERVING

1. Preheat the oven to 190°C (375°F) Mark 5. Peel and finely chop the onion. Heat the oil in a pan, add the onion and cook for about 5 minutes until softened but not coloured. Meanwhile, roughly chop the mushrooms.

2. Add the oatmeal to the onion and cook, stirring, for a further 3-4 minutes, until the oatmeal turns slightly golden.

3. Remove from the heat and stir in the mushrooms, parsley and lemon juice. Season with salt and pepper to taste. Stir in the egg yolk to bind the mixture together.

4. Use a little of the butter to grease an ovenproof dish. Divide the stuffing between the herring, filling the cavities. Lay the fish in the prepared dish and dot with the remaining butter. Cover and bake for 10 minutes. Uncover and cook for a further 5-8 minutes, until the fish flakes easily. Serve immediately.

VARIATION

Use the stuffing to fill mackerel instead of herring. Increase the baking time by about 5 minutes.

TECHNIQUE

Spoon the oatmeal stuffing into the herring cavities, dividing it equally between them.

PAN-FRIED HERRING ROES WITH POTATO PANCAKES

For this quick supper dish all the components can be cooked in the same pan, one after another. Firstly, the pancakes are fried until crisp and golden, then apple slices are sautéed until soft and melting, and finally the herring roes are cooked in butter and lightly seasoned with cayenne pepper. The combination of tastes and textures is quite delicious!

SERVES 4

POTATO PANCAKES
450 g (1 lb) potatoes
½ onion
2 eggs, beaten
30 ml (2 tbsp) plain flour
5 ml (1 tsp) salt
pepper
oil for frying
PAN-FRY
2 eating apples (preferably
   red-skinned)
75 g (3 oz) butter
575 g (1¼ lb) fresh herring
   roes
1.25 ml (¼ tsp) cayenne
   pepper
30 ml (2 tbsp) chopped
   fresh parsley

PREPARATION TIME
10 minutes
COOKING TIME
20 minutes
FREEZING
Not suitable

525 CALS PER SERVING

1. To make the potato pancakes, grate the potatoes fairly coarsely, then squeeze out as much moisture as possible (see technique).

2. Peel and finely chop the onion. Place the grated potatoes in a bowl and add the onion, eggs, flour and salt. Season with pepper and mix well.

3. Heat enough oil in a frying pan (preferably a non-stick one) to cover the base with a thin layer. Put large spoonfuls of the potato mixture into the pan, flattening them down as you do so; they should be roughly 7.5 cm (3 inches) in diameter. Fry for about 3 minutes on each side until golden and crisp. Repeat to make 8 pancakes in total. Remove from the pan and drain on kitchen paper; keep hot.

4. Wipe the frying pan out with kitchen paper. Core the apples and cut into thickish slices. Melt 25 g (1 oz) butter in the pan and when foaming, add the apple slices. Sauté until softened, but still retaining their shape. Remove from the pan and keep warm.

5. Melt the remaining butter in the pan. When it is beginning to turn brown, add the herring roes and sauté for about

5 minutes until lightly golden. Sprinkle with the cayenne and a little salt and pepper.

6. Put two potato pancakes on each warmed serving plate and divide the fried herring roes between the plates. Spoon the pan juices over the roes. Garnish with the apple slices and a sprinkling of chopped parsley.

VARIATION

Cod's roe can be used in place of the herring roe. However, it must be gently poached first, left to cool, then sliced and fried as directed.

TECHNIQUE

To extract as much moisture as possible from the grated potatoes, place them on a clean piece of muslin, bring the corners together and squeeze tightly.

FISH PIE WITH SAFFRON MASH

Here's another favourite with a difference. Chunks of cod, prawns and mussels are cooked in a creamy sauce under a layer of golden coloured saffron-scented mashed potato. The pie is flavoured with fresh dill and tomato, and is guaranteed to become a firm favourite!

SERVES 4-6

SAFFRON MASH
1 kg (2¼ lb) floury potatoes
5 ml (1 tsp) saffron threads
1 garlic clove, peeled
75 g (3 oz) butter, melted
150 ml (¼ pint) single
  cream
150 ml (¼ pint) milk
salt and pepper
PIE FILLING
450 g (1 lb) cod fillet
450 ml (¾ pint) milk
½ onion, sliced
1 bay leaf
225 g (8 oz) tomatoes
175 g (6 oz) cooked shelled
  prawns
175 g (6 oz) cooked shelled
  mussels
15 ml (1 tbsp) chopped
  fresh dill
50 g (2 oz) butter
25 g (1 oz) plain flour

PREPARATION TIME
25 minutes
COOKING TIME
30-35 minutes
FREEZING
Suitable: Provided prawns and
mussels are fresh.

845-550 CALS PER SERVING

1. Preheat the oven to 180°C (350°F) Mark 4. For the saffron mash, peel the potatoes and cut into even-sized chunks. Put them in a pan with enough water to cover, and add the saffron and garlic. Bring to the boil and simmer, covered, until cooked.

2. Drain the potatoes, retaining the saffron and garlic. Add the butter and mash smoothly. Add the cream and milk and beat until light and fluffy. Season with salt and pepper to taste.

3. Meanwhile, lay the cod in an oven-proof dish, pour in the milk and add the onion and bay leaf. Cover and cook in the oven for 20 minutes until the fish is firm. Strain off the milk and reserve.

4. In the meantime, plunge the tomatoes into boiling water for 30 seconds, then refresh in cold water and peel away the skins. Cut into quarters, remove the seeds and roughly chop the flesh.

5. Turn the oven up to 230°C (450°F) Mark 8. Flake the cod into a buttered ovenproof dish. Add the prawns, mussels and tomatoes. Scatter over the dill.

6. Melt 25 g (1 oz) butter in a pan, add the flour and cook for 30 seconds. Stir in the reserved milk, and cook, stirring, until thickened. Season with salt and pepper and pour over the fish.

7. Spoon the saffron mash on top of the fish mixture, covering it completely. Dot with the remaining butter and bake in the oven for 10-15 minutes until nicely browned on top.

NOTE: If using frozen prawns and mussels, defrost thoroughly in the refrigerator overnight; drain well before adding to the cod.

VARIATION

Omit the saffron. Flavour the mashed potato with some finely chopped spring onions or chopped fresh herbs, such as dill, tarragon and chervil.

TECHNIQUE

Beat the cream and milk into the saffron mashed potato, until light and fluffy.

COD, AUBERGINE AND SWEET PEPPER CASSEROLE

This is the sort of dish you can imagine eating in a little fishing village, somewhere in Spain or Italy. Tender chunks of cod are gently cooked with aubergines, peppers, onions and garlic in a rich tomato sauce, flavoured with oregano. All you need to accompany this dish is some crusty bread to mop up the delicious juices. A glass of chilled red wine wouldn't go amiss either!

SERVES 4

2 onions
2 garlic cloves
1 large aubergine
1 red pepper
1 yellow pepper
575 -700 g (1¼ – 1½ lb)
   thick-cut skinless cod fillet
salt and pepper
75 ml (5 tbsp) plain flour
60 ml (4 tbsp) olive oil
400 g (14 oz) canned
   chopped tomatoes
15 ml (1 tbsp) tomato
   purée
125 ml (4 fl oz) light red
   wine
15 ml (1 tbsp) chopped
   fresh oregano

PREPARATION TIME
20 minutes
COOKING TIME
About 40 minutes
FREEZING
Not suitable

415 CALS PER SERVING

1. Peel and roughly chop the onions and garlic. Peel the aubergine and cut into 4 cm (1½ inch) cubes. Halve the peppers, remove the core and seeds, then cut into thick strips.

2. Cut the cod into 5 cm (2 inch) pieces. Season with salt and pepper, and dust with flour. Heat the oil in a shallow flameproof casserole or heavy-based pan, add the fish and fry briefly, turning until golden on all sides. Remove from the pan and set aside.

3. Add the onions, garlic, aubergine and peppers to the pan and sauté for about 10 minutes until softened. Add the tomatoes, tomato purée and red wine. Season with salt and pepper. Cook, covered, for 20 minutes.

4. Add the cod and oregano. Cook, uncovered, for 10 minutes, or until the cod is tender. Serve immediately.

VARIATION

Any prepared fish can be added to this casserole. If you prefer, use a mixture of cod with other varieties such as monk-fish, prawns, squid, clams etc.

TECHNIQUE

Fry the pieces of cod, turning until golden on all sides.

SEAFOOD RISOTTO

For an authentic risotto, you need to use arborio rice. This is the classic Italian risotto rice which yields a delicious creamy texture. For convenience this recipe used ready-prepared mixed frozen seafood, which is available in packets from larger supermarkets. However, you can, of course, use a mixture of fresh mussels, squid and shelled prawns, and prepare them yourself if you prefer. Finely grated lemon rind and chopped fresh tarragon are added to enhance the flavours of the seafood, and sun-dried tomato paste gives the dish a pretty speckled appearance.

SERVES 4

1 onion
2 garlic cloves
60 ml (4 tbsp) sunflower oil
225 g (8 oz) arborio rice
100 ml (3 ½ fl oz) dry white
   wine
1.5-1.6 litres (2¼-2½ pints)
   hot fish stock
300 g (10 oz) packet frozen
   mixed seafood, thawed
grated rind of 1 small
   lemon
30 ml (2 tbsp) sun-dried
   tomato paste
15 ml (1 tbsp) chopped
   fresh tarragon
salt and pepper

PREPARATION TIME
10 minutes
COOKING TIME
30 minutes
FREEZING
Not suitable

420 CALS PER SERVING

1. Peel and finely chop the onion; crush the garlic. Heat the oil in a heavy-based pan, add the onion and garlic and cook until softened. Add the rice and cook, stirring, for about 1 minute.

2. Add the wine and stir until it is absorbed. Add 150 ml (¼ pint) of the hot stock, and cook, stirring constantly, until the liquid is absorbed by the rice. Continue adding stock in 150 ml (¼ pint) quantities, until you have used half of it. This should take about 10 minutes, by which time the rice should be about half cooked.

3. Stir in the seafood and cook for 2-3 minutes. Continue adding the stock as before, until the rice is cooked. It should be *al dente* or tender but with a firm bite, and holding together in a creamy mass. (You may not need to add all of the stock.)

4. Stir in the lemon rind, sun-dried tomato paste and the chopped tarragon. Season with salt and pepper to taste. Leave to stand off the heat for a few minutes to allow the flavours to mingle. Serve warm.

VARIATION

If preferred, make the risotto with one type of seafood only, such as prawns or mussels. Vary the herbs if you like; use fresh dill, parsley or chervil instead of tarragon.

TECHNIQUE

Add the stock to the rice 150 ml (¼ pint) at a time, stirring constantly. As each quantity is absorbed by the rice, add the next.

Braised Cod Boulangère

Thick cod fillets are pan-fried briefly to give them a golden hue, then baked on a bed of sliced potatoes and onions, flavoured with herbs and moistened with stock. This is the perfect supper dish – easy to prepare and cook, and can be brought to the table in the dish it's cooked in. Serve with a green vegetable; fresh peas, when in season, are the perfect accompaniment.

SERVES 4

700 g (1½ lb) potatoes
1 onion
75 g (3 oz) butter
salt and pepper
few fresh thyme sprigs
300 ml (½ pint) chicken stock
4 thick cod fillets, each about 150 g (5 oz)
snipped chives, to garnish

PREPARATION TIME
10 minutes
COOKING TIME
1 hour
FREEZING
Not suitable

395 CALS PER SERVING

1. Preheat the oven to 190°C (375°F) Mark 5. Peel the potatoes and onion, then slice both thinly and as evenly as possible.

2. Use 25 g (1 oz) of the butter to grease an ovenproof dish. Layer the potatoes and onion alternately in the dish, sprinkling each layer with salt, pepper and thyme. Dot with half of the remaining butter. Pour in the stock and bake in the oven for 40-50 minutes.

3. Melt the remaining butter in a non-stick frying pan, add the cod fillets and fry briefly until golden on both sides.

4. Place the fish on top of the potatoes. Cover the dish and return to the oven for a further 10-15 minutes. The fish should be firm, but tender; check by prising the flesh away from the bone – if it comes away easily, the fish is ready.

5. Sprinkle the dish with the chives and serve immediately.

VARIATION

Use fillets of haddock, sole or whiting instead of cod.

TECHNIQUE

Layer the potatoes and onions in a greased ovenproof dish, sprinkling each layer with salt, pepper and thyme.

SMOKED HADDOCK FISH CAKES WITH PARSLEY SAUCE

Homemade fish cakes are always popular – a little time-consuming to make perhaps, but well worth the effort. I usually make double the quantity, and freeze half for another meal. These fish cakes include bacon pieces and have a subtle smoky flavour. A parsley sauce is the traditional accompaniment.

SERVES 4

350 g (12 oz) undyed
    smoked haddock
450 g (1 lb) potatoes
salt and pepper
6 rashers streaky bacon,
    derinded
4 spring onions, trimmed
25 g (1 oz) butter
15 ml (1 tbsp) lemon juice
15 ml (1 tbsp) chopped
    fresh parsley
1 egg, beaten
50 g (2 oz) fresh white
    breadcrumbs (see note)
oil for frying
PARSLEY SAUCE
300 ml (½ pint) milk
1 slice onion
1 bay leaf
6 peppercorns
20 g (¾ oz) butter
20 ml (1½ tbsp) plain flour
50 g (2 oz) chopped fresh
    parsley
25 g (1 oz) butter

PREPARATION TIME
20 minutes
COOKING TIME
35-40 minutes
FREEZING
Suitable

530 CALS PER SERVING

1. Place the haddock in a pan and add sufficient water to just cover. Bring to the boil, lower heat and poach gently for 15-20 minutes, until the fish flakes.

2. Meanwhile, peel the potatoes, cut into even-sized pieces and cook in boiling salted water until tender. Drain well and mash until smooth.

3. Preheat the grill and grill the bacon until just brown, but not crispy. Chop into small pieces.

4. Drain the fish and flake, discarding any bones and skin. Mix the fish with the mashed potatoes and bacon.

5. Chop the spring onions. Melt the butter in a small pan, add the spring onions and cook until beginning to soften. Add to the fish mixture, with the lemon juice, parsley and seasoning. Add just enough beaten egg to bind the mixture; it must be firm enough to shape.

6. With floured hands, shape the mixture into 8 cakes. Brush with beaten egg and coat in the breadcrumbs. Chill in the refrigerator for 30 minutes.

7. To make the parsley sauce, put the milk in a pan with the onion, bay leaf and peppercorns. Bring to the boil, turn off

the heat, cover and leave to infuse for 10 minutes. Melt the butter in a pan, add the flour and cook, stirring, for 1-2 minutes. Remove from the heat and strain in the hot milk, whisking well. Bring to the boil, stirring until the sauce thickens. Stir in the chopped parsley, butter and seasoning to taste. Keep warm.

8. Heat the oil in a frying pan and shallow fry the fish cakes in batches if necessary, for about 5 minutes on each side, until golden and crisp. Drain on kitchen paper, then serve immediately, with the parsley sauce.

NOTE: For convenience, coat the fish cakes in ready-prepared dried breadcrumbs rather than fresh ones.

TECHNIQUE

Dust your hands with flour, then shape the mixture into 8 cakes, each about 2.5 cm (1 inch) thick.

SEAFOOD AND MELON SALAD WITH GINGER LIME DRESSING

For this clean, fresh tasting salad, prawns, mussels and squid are combined with fragrant melon in a piquant dressing of lime juice, fresh ginger and chilli. Serve it on a bed of pretty mixed salad leaves as part of a buffet, or piled into scallop shells as a starter.

SERVES 4

250 g (9 oz) packet mixed
    seafood (fresh or frozen
    and thawed)
1 ripe Charentais melon
2 ripe tomatoes
15-30 ml (1-2 tbsp) chopped
    fresh coriander or parsley
DRESSING
15 g (½ oz) fresh root
    ginger
1 red chilli
25 ml (1 fl oz) sunflower or
    peanut oil
juice of 2 limes
grated rind of ½ lime
pinch of salt
15 ml (1 tbsp) chopped
    fresh coriander
TO GARNISH
lettuce leaves
coriander sprigs
lime wedges

PREPARATION TIME
15 minutes, plus marinating
COOKING TIME
Nil
FREEZING Not suitable

140 CALS PER SERVING

1. First make the dressing. Peel the ginger and shred finely or cut into very fine julienne strips. Halve the chilli lengthwise, remove the seeds, then cut into very fine strips. In a bowl, whisk together the oil and lime juice until thoroughly combined. Stir in the lime rind, ginger, chilli, salt and chopped coriander.

2. Place the seafood in a shallow dish and pour over the dressing. Mix gently, cover and leave to marinate in the refrigerator for 1-2 hours.

3. Halve the melon, scoop out and discard the seeds. Cut the melon into 8 wedges, then cut the flesh away from the skin and slice into chunks.

4. Immerse the tomatoes in a bowl of boiling water for 30 seconds, then refresh in cold water. Peel away the skins. Quarter the tomatoes and remove the seeds.

5. Add the melon, tomato and coriander or parsley to the marinated seafood and toss gently to thoroughly combine all the ingredients. Serve on a bed of lettuce leaves, garnished with sprigs of coriander and lime wedges.

NOTE: If you want to make the salad in advance, prepare up to step 4, keeping the melon and tomato separate. Mix together just before serving.

TECHNIQUE

Wearing rubber gloves to prevent skin irritation, halve the chilli lengthwise and remove the seeds.

SCALLOP, BROAD BEAN AND BACON SALAD

Tiny queen scallops are briefly cooked, and mixed with broad beans, crispy bacon pieces and fresh, young spinach leaves. The salad is then drizzled with a creamy mustard dressing. If you buy scallops in their shells, scrub and retain some of the shells to use as a garnish (as shown).

SERVES 4

175 g (6 oz) lardons (bacon pieces)

450 g (1 lb) shelled queen scallops (see page 5)

150 g (5 oz) shelled broad beans

225 g (8 oz) young spinach leaves

DRESSING

90 ml (6 tbsp) light olive oil

15 ml (1 tbsp) lemon juice

5 ml (1 tsp) wholegrain mustard

15-30 ml (1-2 tbsp) chopped fresh dill or parsley

salt and pepper

PREPARATION TIME
10-20 minutes
COOKING TIME
10-12 minutes
FREEZING
Not suitable

625 CALS PER SERVING

1. First make the dressing. Put the oil, lemon juice, mustard and dill or parsley in a screw-topped jar and shake vigorously to combine. Season with salt and pepper to taste.

2. Put the lardons or bacon pieces in a heavy-based frying pan over a moderate heat and fry them in their own fat until crispy. Remove with a slotted spoon and drain on kitchen paper. Set the frying pan over a high heat, add the scallops and sauté for 1-2 minutes. Remove from the pan and allow to cool.

3. Cook the broad beans in boiling salted water for 5-6 minutes. Drain and refresh under cold running water. Drain thoroughly and slip the broad beans out of their skins, if preferred.

4. Wash and dry the spinach thoroughly, if necessary. Place in a salad bowl with the bacon, scallops and broad beans and toss to mix the ingredients together. Just before serving, drizzle the dressing over the salad and toss lightly.

NOTE: It isn't essential to skin the broad beans but the outer skins can be a little tough and the beans are a pretty vibrant green underneath.

VARIATION

Use fresh peas or mangetouts instead of broad beans.

TECHNIQUE

Add the scallops to the frying pan and sauté over a high heat for 1-2 minutes.

PRAWN AND GLASS NOODLE SALAD

A very pretty dish, inspired by the salad I always choose at my favourite Thai restaurant. The glass noodles, or cellophane noodles as they are sometimes referred to, are made from mung beans. They are as thin as pasta vermicelli and have a transparent quality, which makes them an attractive and unusual addition to a salad. Serve as a starter, or as a light lunch dish.

SERVES 4

50 g (2 oz) glass (or cellophane) noodles
75 g (3 oz) shiitake
  mushrooms
1 large carrot
1 large courgette
12 large cooked prawns,
  shelled (see page 6)
DRESSING
2 garlic cloves
15 ml (1 tbsp) light soy
  sauce
30 ml (2 tbsp) sugar
15 ml (1 tbsp) wine vinegar
15 ml (1 tbsp) sesame oil
1 red chilli
TO GARNISH
15 ml (1 tbsp) toasted
  sesame seeds
30 ml (2 tbsp) chopped
  fresh coriander

PREPARATION TIME
15 minutes
COOKING TIME
1 minute
FREEZING
Not suitable

170 CALS PER SERVING

1. First make the dressing. Crush the garlic and mix with the soy sauce, sugar, wine vinegar and sesame oil in a small bowl. Cut the chilli in half lengthwise, remove the seeds, then cut into very fine strips. Mix into the dressing.

2. Cut the noodles into 10 cm (4 inch) lengths. Cook in boiling water for 1 minute or according to packet instructions. Drain thoroughly and refresh under cold running water. Drain again.

3. Trim the mushrooms and slice finely. Add to the dressing and mix thoroughly.

4. Cut the carrot and courgette into fine julienne, or matchstick strips.

5. Place the noodles in a bowl and add the mushrooms with the dressing, the carrot and courgette julienne, and the prawns. Toss the salad well to combine all the ingredients. Sprinkle with the sesame seeds and garnish with chopped coriander to serve.

VARIATIONS

• Use other cooked seafood such as squid, mussels or crab meat, instead of prawns.
• For a warm salad, do not refresh the cooked noodles with cold water. Simply drain and toss the hot noodles with the other ingredients.

TECHNIQUE

Cut the carrot and courgette into julienne strips, using a sharp knife.

SEARED TUNA WITH A SWEET SOUR MARINADE

The freshest tuna is cooked over a very high heat to seal the outside and create a crisp exterior, while the inside of the fish remains raw. It is then cut into thin slices and marinated in olive oil, lemon juice and balsamic vinegar, with pine nuts and raisins. This recipe combines Japanese and Italian influences. The secret of success lies in the tuna being as fresh as possible, and the pan being as hot as possible.

SERVES 4

450 g (1 lb) piece fresh tuna
    fillet, about 4-5 cm (2-2½
    inches) thick
60 ml (4 tbsp) olive oil
salt and pepper
MARINADE
175 ml (6 fl oz) extra-virgin
    olive oil
juice of 1 lemon
30 ml (2 tbsp) balsamic
    vinegar
3 cloves
1 bay leaf
45 ml (3 tbsp) pine nuts
45 ml (3 tbsp) raisins
15 ml (1 tbsp) sugar
1.25 ml (¼ tsp) dried chilli
    flakes
TO SERVE
175 g (6 oz) young spinach
    or rocket leaves

PREPARATION TIME
10 minutes, plus marinating
COOKING TIME
6 minutes
FREEZING
Not suitable

385-425 CALS PER SERVING

1. Slice the tuna fillet in half, then rub with a little olive oil and season with salt and pepper. Heat the remaining oil in a heavy-based frying pan, or cast-iron griddle. When it is very hot, add the tuna, one piece at a time. Cook over a very high heat for about 1 minute on each side, including the ends, using two wooden spoons to turn the fish. Make sure it's well browned and verging on crisp on the outside. Remove from the pan and allow to cool, then wrap in cling film and refrigerate for 30 minutes.

2. To prepare the marinade, in a small bowl mix together the olive oil, lemon juice, balsamic vinegar, cloves, bay leaf, pine nuts, raisins, sugar and chilli flakes.

3. When the tuna is chilled and firm, unwrap and, using a very sharp knife, cut into thin slices, about 5 mm (¼ inch) thick. Lay the tuna slices, overlapping, in a shallow glass or earthenware dish and pour on the marinade. Cover and leave to marinate in the refrigerator for several hours, or overnight if possible.

4. Take the tuna out of the refrigerator an hour or so before serving, to let it come to room temperature. Serve the tuna slices on a bed of spinach or rocket with the marinade spooned over.

VARIATION

Use fresh salmon in place of the tuna.

TECHNIQUE

Cook the tuna in a heavy-based pan over a high heat until well browned on the outside, but still raw inside.

LIME MARINATED HALIBUT WITH AVOCADO AND RED ONION SALSA

This recipe is based in the famous Mexican dish of ceviche – raw fish marinated in citrus juices. The acid from the fruit 'cooks' the fish, but retains the texture, keeping it moist. Most white fish can be used, and scallops work well too. Again, this recipe relies on the freshest of fish for its success. It make a splendid starter, served with toasted corn bread or warm soft tortillas.

SERVES 4

575 g (1¼ lb) halibut
juice of 1 orange
juice of 5 limes
SALSA
1 red pepper
1 red chilli
1 small red onion
1 beef tomato
1 small avocado
60 ml (4 tbsp) chopped
   fresh coriander
30 ml (2 tbsp) chopped
   fresh parsley
1.25 ml (¼ tsp) salt
pepper

PREPARATION TIME
10 minutes, plus marinating
COOKING TIME
Nil
FREEZING
Not suitable

210 CALS PER SERVING

1. Remove any skin and bones from the fish, and cut into bite-size pieces. Place in a bowl with the orange juice and lime juice. Turn the fish and make sure that it is all covered with citrus juice. Cover the bowl and leave to marinate in the refrigerator for at least 8 hours, or preferably overnight.

2. To make the salsa, halve the pepper, remove the core and seeds, then dice the flesh. Cut the chilli in half lengthways, remove the seeds and chop very finely. Peel and dice the red onion. Mix all these ingredients together in a bowl.

3. Immerse the tomato in a small bowl of boiling water, leave for 30 seconds, then refresh in cold water. Peel away the skin. Cut the tomato into quarters, remove the seeds, then dice the flesh.

4. Cut the avocado in half, remove the stone and peel away the skin. Cut the flesh into dice. Add to the onion mixture with the tomato, coriander, parsley, salt and pepper to taste. Mix well.

5. Serve the marinated fish on individual plates topped, with a spoonful of salsa.

NOTE: If a smoother sauce is preferred, the salsa ingredients can be puréed in a blender or food processor.

TECHNIQUE

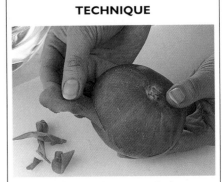

Immerse the beef tomato in boiling water for 30 seconds, refresh in cold water, then peel away the skin. (It should lift off easily).

SMOKED MUSSEL AND PASTA SALAD

This colourful salad is crammed full of delicious ingredients. An unusual dressing of puréed roasted pepper, olive oil and garlic gives the pasta a wonderful flavour, which is enhanced by the smokiness of the mussels. Grilled salad onions are included too, for added flavour and texture. If possible, make the salad in advance to allow the flavours time to mature, but add the avocado just before serving.

SERVES 4

2 red peppers
8 salad onions
90 ml (3 fl oz) olive oil
1 garlic clove
10 ml (2 tsp) red wine
    vinegar
salt and pepper
350 g (12 oz) dried pasta
    shapes, such as shells,
    tubes or bows
125 g (4 oz) fresh or frozen
    peas
two 105 g (3½ oz) cans
    smoked mussels, drained
30 ml (2 tbsp) chopped
    fresh parsley
1 avocado
TO GARNISH
parsley sprigs

PREPARATION TIME
15 minutes
COOKING TIME
15-20 minutes
FREEZING
Not suitable

660 CALS PER SERVING

1. Cut the peppers into quarters, then remove the core and seeds. Peel the onions and cut into quarters.

2. Preheat the grill. Place the quartered onions and peppers, skin-side up, in the grill pan and drizzle with 15 ml (1 tbsp) of the olive oil. Grill until the pepper skins are charred and the onions are nicely browned. (You may need to remove the onions before the peppers.) Place the peppers in a bowl and cover with a plate; the steam created will help to loosen the skins.

3. When the peppers are cool enough to handle, peel away the skins. Place half the peppers in a blender or food processor. Peel and roughly chop the garlic; add to the blender with the remaining oil and the vinegar. Work to a purée, and season with salt and pepper to taste.

4. Cook the pasta in a large pan of boiling salted water according to the packet instructions until *al dente* (tender but firm to the bite). About 5 minutes before the end of the cooking time, add the peas. Drain the cooked pasta and peas, then immediately refresh under cold running water. Drain thoroughly.

5. Cut the remaining pepper into strips. Halve the avocado, remove the stone and skin, then cut into chunks.

6. Transfer the pasta and peas to a large bowl, add the pepper dressing and toss well. Add the pepper strips, grilled onions, mussels, chopped parsley and avocado. Toss gently to combine all the ingredients and check the seasoning. Serve garnished with parsley.

NOTE: Canned smoked mussels are available from large supermarkets and delicatessens. You will find them alongside tinned tuna, sardines etc. Smoked oysters are a delicious alternative.

TECHNIQUE

Put the grilled peppers in a covered bowl until cool enough to handle, then peel away the skins.